GRADE-2 FUNDAMENTAL MATHS

Fun-filled Activities

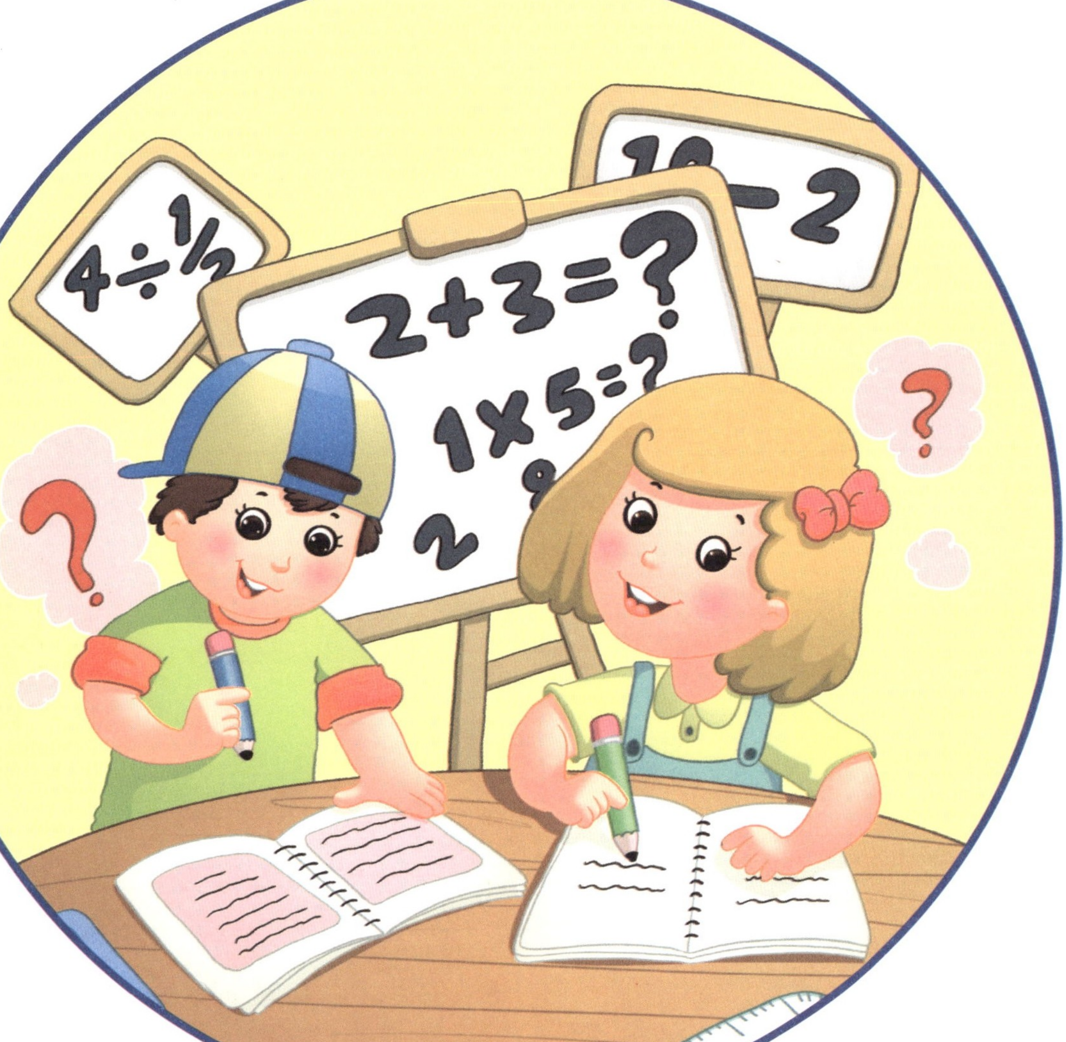

Om KIDZ

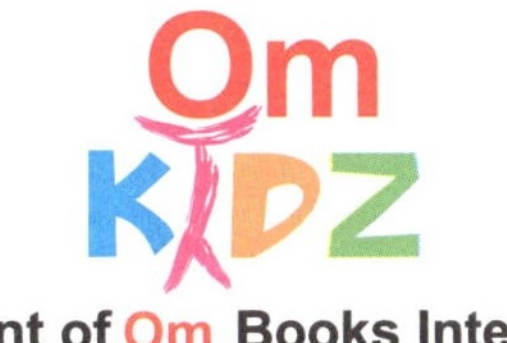

An imprint of Om Books International

Numbers to 999

Study the grid carefully.

10	20	30	40	50	60	70	80	90	100
110	120	130	140	150	160	170	180	190	200
210	220	230	240	250	260		280	290	300
310	320	330	340	350	360	370	380	390	400
410		430	440	450	460	470	480	490	500
510	520	530	540		560	570	580	590	600
610	620	630	640	650	660	670	680	690	
710	720	730	740	750	760		780	790	800
810	820	830	840	850	860	870	880	890	900
910		930	940	950	960	970	980	990	1000

1. Write the 6 missing numbers in the grid.

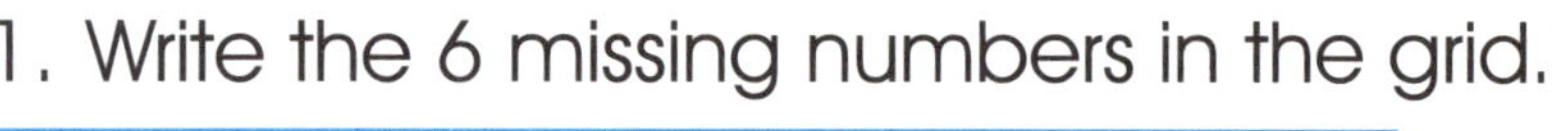

2. Write the numbers between 520 to 530.

3. 5 more than 270.

4. 10 less than 580.

5. Write the numbers 10 more than 500, 760, 910, 650.

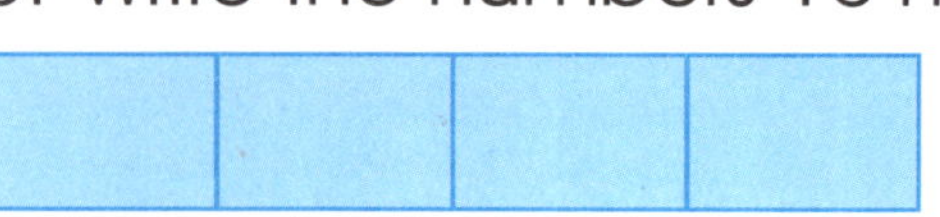

Modelling Numbers

Count the blocks and write the number. Also name the matching room.

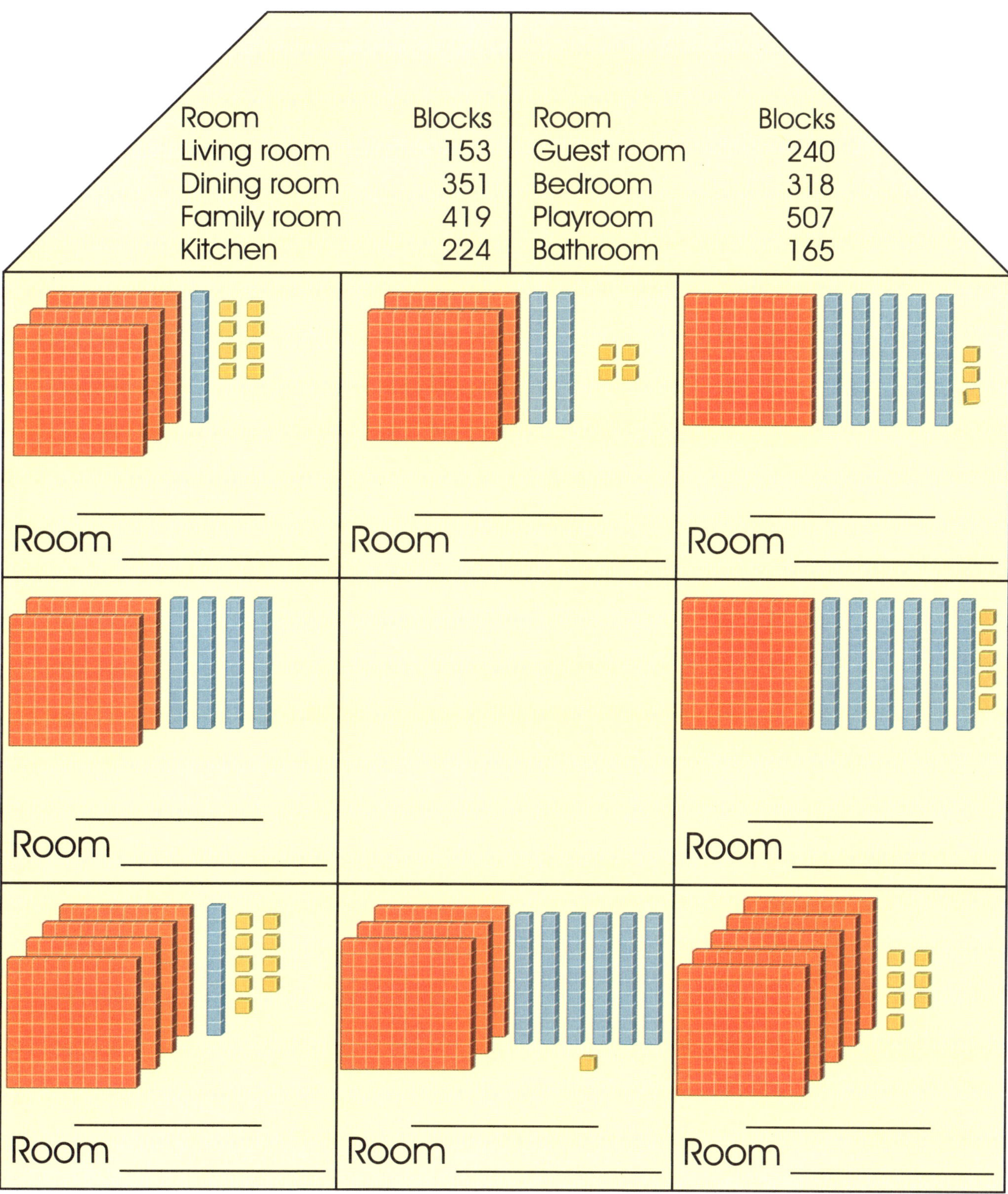

Room	Blocks	Room	Blocks
Living room	153	Guest room	240
Dining room	351	Bedroom	318
Family room	419	Playroom	507
Kitchen	224	Bathroom	165

Modelling Numbers

In each row, circle the blocks to show the number.

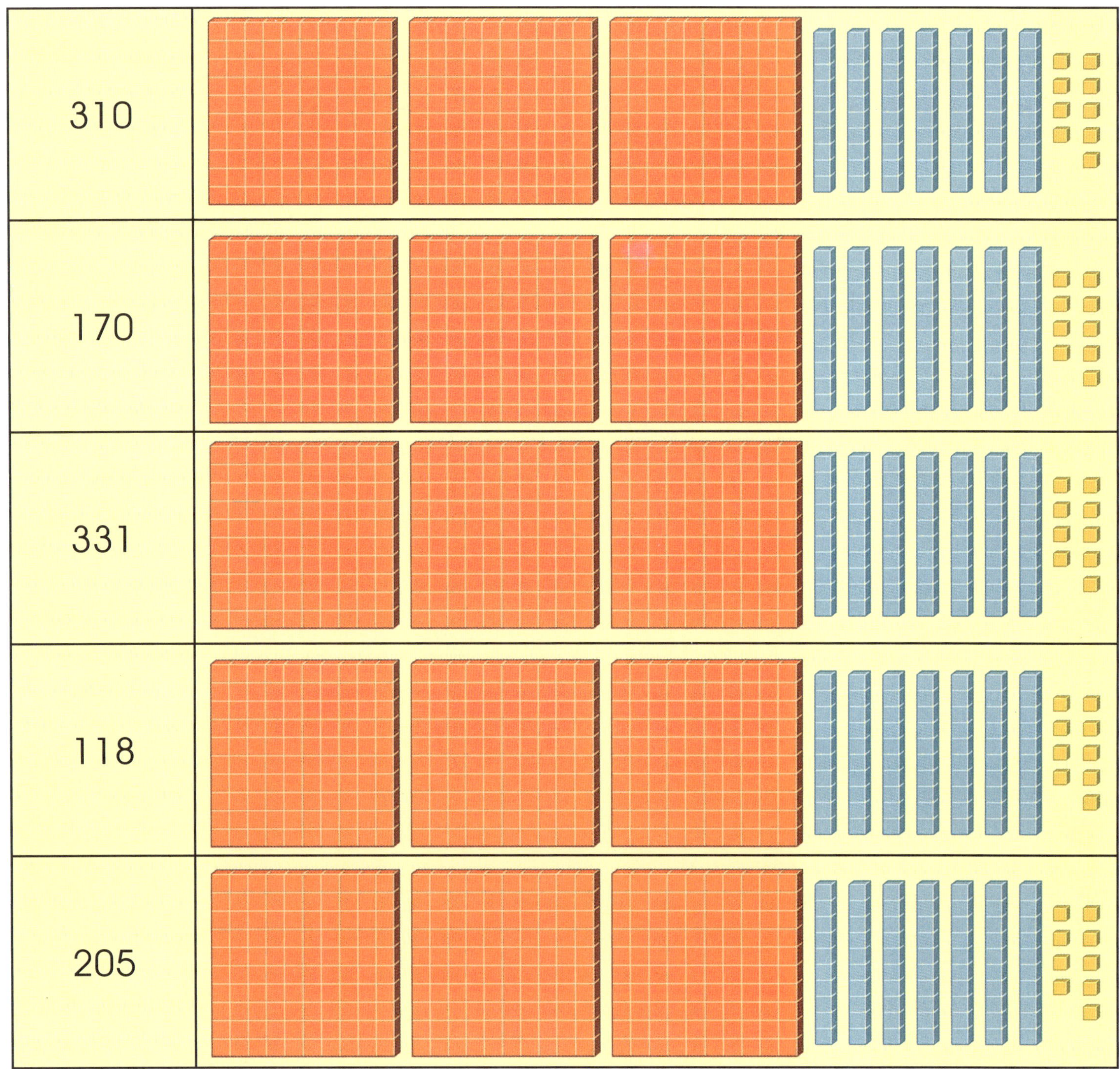

CHALLENGE

Use the digits of the numbers given above and write 5 new numbers. Use a digit only once.

Hundreds, Tens and Ones

6 hundreds 4 tens and 5 ones

Write the number you see on each abacus.

① H T O

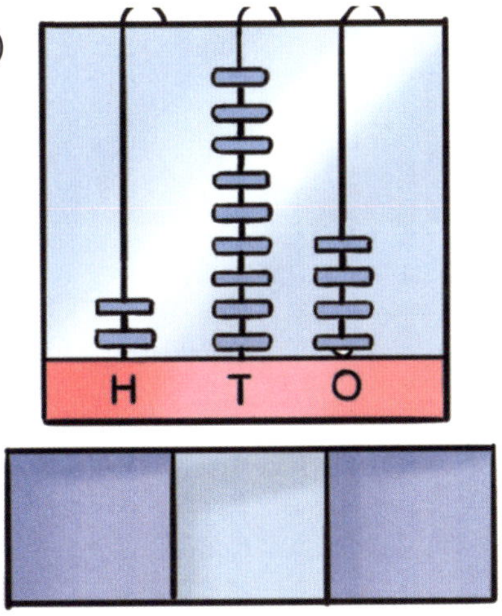

② H T O

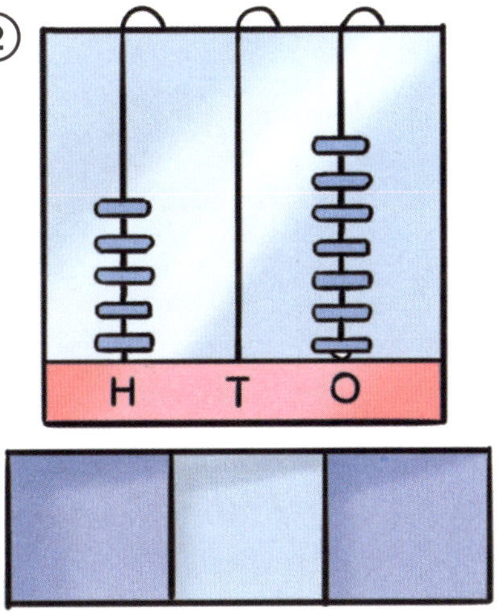

③ H T O

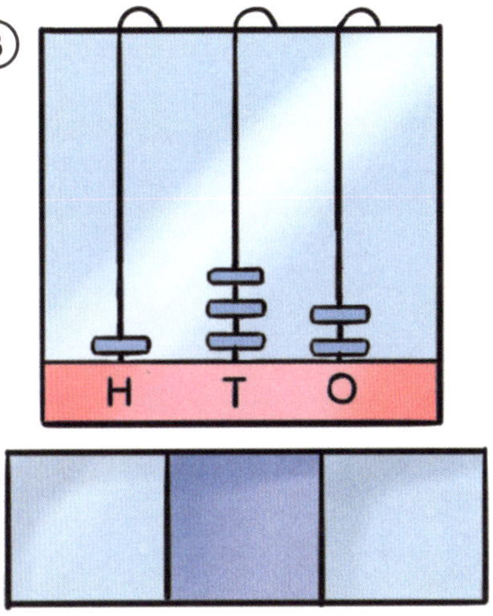

④ H T O

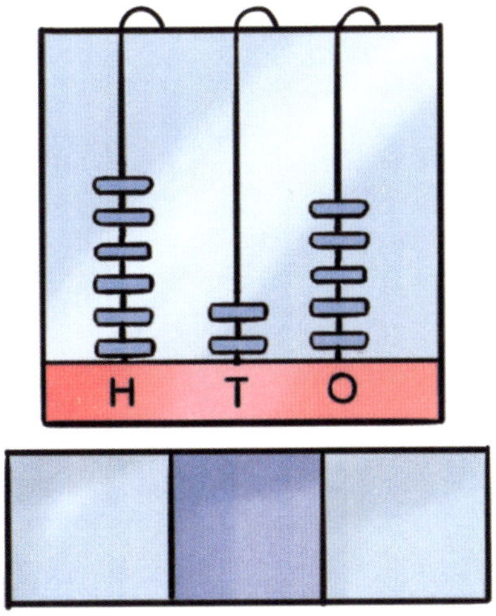

⑤ H T O

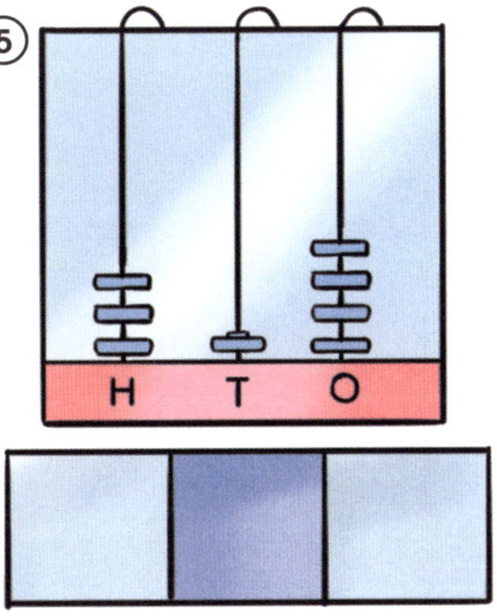

⑥ H T O

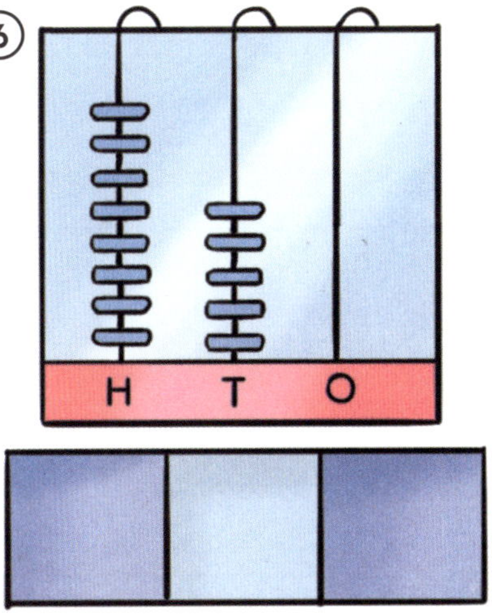

Before, Between and After

Write the numbers and complete the table.

Before		After
	339	
	517	
	208	
	899	
	700	

	Between	
399		401
628		630
147		149
512		514
765		767
771		773

209
518
338
340
516
207
701
699
898
900
148
513
400
629
766
772

CHALLENGE

Make a grid of numbers such that each row adds up to 540.

Place Value

Place value is the position of a digit in a number.

563 – The place value of 6 in 563 is 6 tens.

563
6 tens

Write the value of each underlined digit. Use the help box.

1. 38 ______
2. 532 ______
3. 460 ______
4. 139 ______
5. 740 ______
6. 834 ______
7. 559 ______
8. 419 ______
9. 475 ______
10. 809 ______
11. 928 ______
12. 489 ______
13. 315 ______
14. 922 ______
15. 601 ______
16. 657 ______
17. 495 ______
18. 648 ______

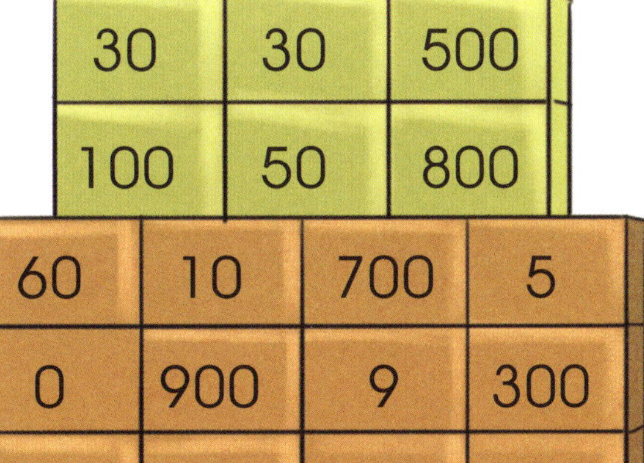

Place Value

Read each clue and find the 3-digit number hidden in the picture. Circle the number and write on the line.

1. There is a 8 in hundreds place and 3 in the tens place. 843
2. There is a 4 in the hundreds place. The other two digits are the same. ________
3. The same digit is in hundreds place and the ones place. ________
4. There is a 6 in the tens place. The sum of the other two digits is 5. ________
5. There is a 9 in the ones place. ________
6. There is a 7 in the hundreds place. ________
7. There is a 4 in the tens place. The sum of the three digits is 16. ________
8. There is a 5 in the tens place. ________

Expanded Form of Numbers

Expanded form is a way to write a number that shows the place value for each place.

100	+	**20**	+	**3**
↑		↑		↑
Hundred		Tens		Ones

Write the expanded form of each number.

1. 487 = __________ + __________ + __________
2. 329 = __________ + __________ + __________
3. 892 = __________ + __________ + __________
4. 278 = __________ + __________ + __________
5. 165 = __________ + __________ + __________
6. 723 = __________ + __________ + __________
7. 735 = __________ + __________ + __________
8. 818 = __________ + __________ + __________
9. 695 = __________ + __________ + __________
10. 224 = __________ + __________ + __________

CHALLENGE

Which number is smaller
600+90+8 or 689? Explain how?

Expanded Form of Numbers

Write each number for the expanded form.

1. 400+60+9 = ________
2. 600+70+8 = ________
3. 900+50+4 = ________
4. 800+0+9 = ________
5. 500+10+4 = ________
6. 600+20+9 = ________
7. 100+80+0 = ________
8. 700+50+4 = ________
9. 300+80+8 = ________
10. 500+80+1 = ________
11. 200+70+3 = ________
12. 400+50+5 = ________
13. 100+90+9 = ________
14. 700+0+4 = ________

CHALLENGE

How many different even and odd numbers can you make using numbers 3, 4, 5? Answer without actually making the numbers. Now make numbers and cross check.

Expanded Form of Numbers

Write each number to its matching expanded form.

1. 7 hundreds
   6 tens =
   4 ones

2. 5 hundreds
   3 tens =
   6 ones

3. 8 hundreds
   1 ten =
   8 ones

4. 9 hundreds
   2 tens =
   3 ones

5. 4 hundreds
   3 tens =
   8 ones

6. 8 hundreds
   3 tens =
   9 ones

7. 5 hundreds
   0 tens =
   3 ones

8. 6 hundreds
   9 tens =
   7 ones

503	818	697	923
438	764	839	536

Comparing Numbers

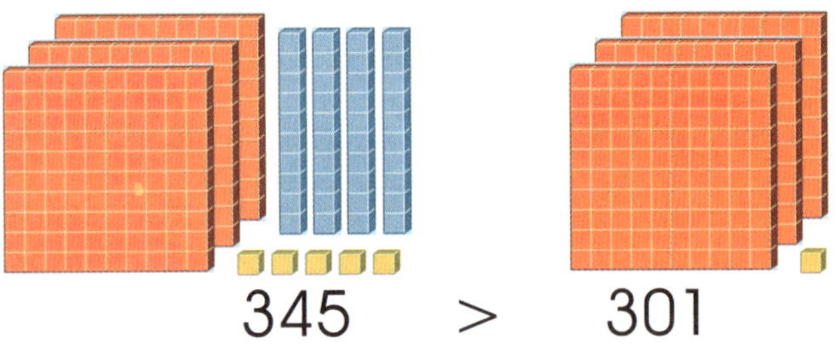

The symbol $>$ points to the number that is less.

$345 > 301$ or $301 < 345$

Write the number for each group. Compare the numbers with $>$, $<$ or $=$.

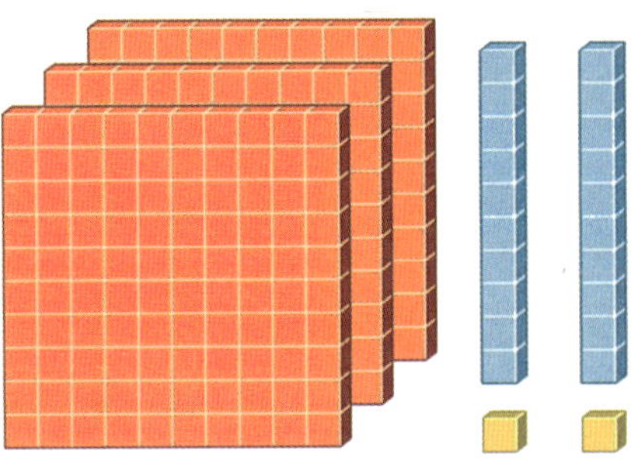

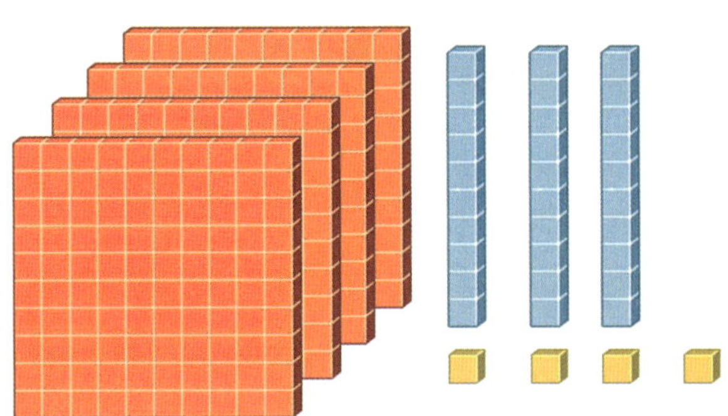

____

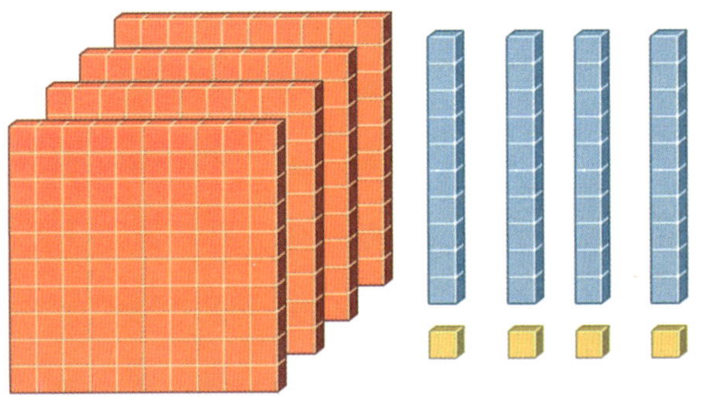

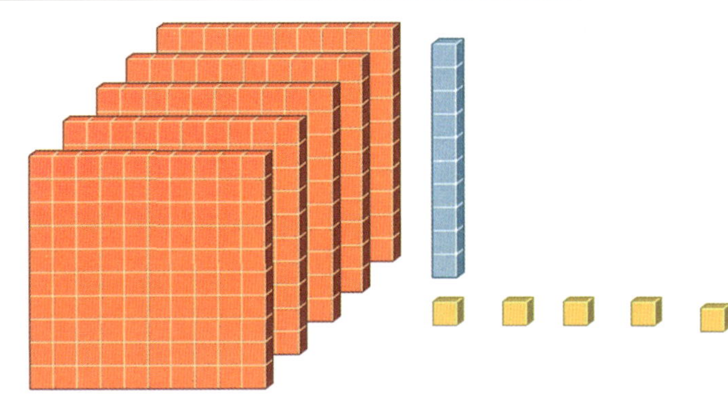

____

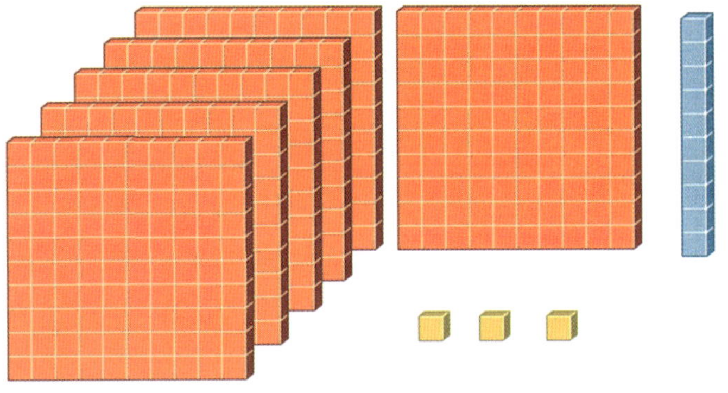

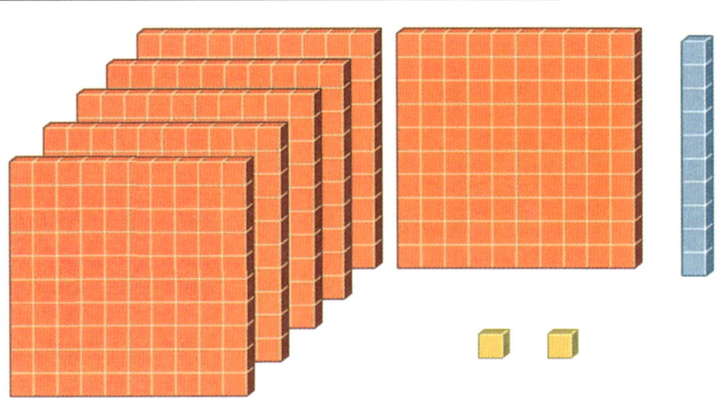

____

Comparing Numbers

Circle the matching number to make the comparison true. Write it on the line.

______ > 335 271 411 126	______ = 809 796 334 809	745 > ______ 816 927 612
753 > ______ 886 522 935	527 < ______ 421 891 344	______ > 241 254 457 119
______ < 651 625 894 753	817 > ______ 998 218 827	______ = 976 220 976 429
______ > 784 658 998 218	______ < 876 786 966 899	475 > ______ 980 337 567

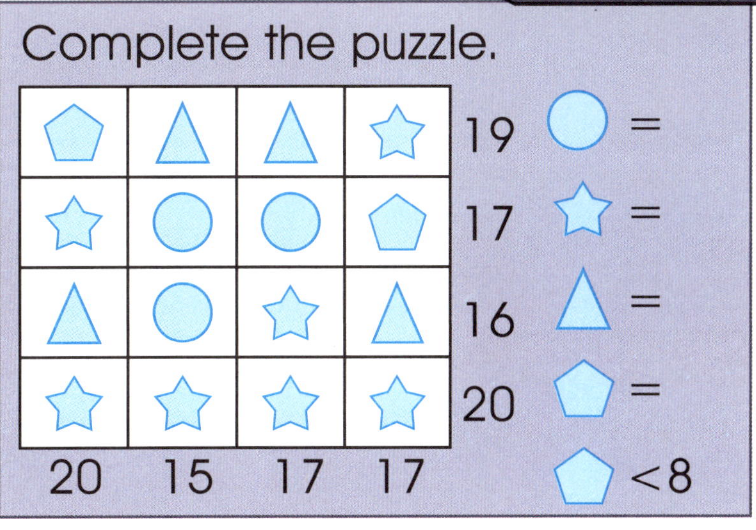

Comparing Numbers

Decide whether each number sentence is true.

Colour the matching star.

		YES	NO
1.	3 hundreds + 8 tens + 9 ones > 398		
2.	748 = 7 hundreds + 4 tens + 8 ones		
3.	2 hundreds + 6 ones = 260		
4.	629 < 6 hundreds + 2 hundreds + 9 ones		
5.	8 hundreds + 6 tens + 1 one > 8 hundreds + 1 ten and 8 ones		
6.	9 hundreds + 5 tens + 6 ones > 953		
7.	5 hundreds + 8 tens + 0 ones = 508		
8.	4 hundreds + 3 tens + 2 ones < 443		

CHALLENGE

Using the numbers 7, 5, 4 make as many numbers as you can. Then make a chart comparing all these numbers.

Ordering Numbers

Read each set of numbers. Write the numbers in order from the least to the greatest.

Writing Number Words

Write number words for these given numbers.

1. 679 ____________________

2. 342 ____________________

3. 908 ____________________

4. 556 ____________________

5. 876 ____________________

6. 259 ____________________

7. 445 ____________________

8. 178 ____________________

9. 784 ____________________

10. 119 ____________________

Counting in 5s and 10s

Write 5 more than:

1. 20 ______ 2. 30 ______ 3. 45 ______

4. 0 ______ 5. 15 ______ 6. 40 ______

7. 25 ______ 8. 10 ______ 9. 50 ______

10. 35 ______ 11. 55 ______ 12. 5 ______

Write the above numbers in order from least to greatest.

The numbers on the cards below are to be counted in 10s. Put the numbers in order from largest to smallest and complete the number grid. Write the missing numbers if any.

105	215	245	305	265	195	235
275	205	165	115	155	185	225

Counting in 2s, 3s, 4s, 5s and 10s

Fill in the missing letters to complete the set of numbers. Write the rule you used.

1. ____, ____, 130, 140

2. 315, 320, 325, ____

3. 223, 226, ____, 232, ____

4. ____, 565, 570, ____, 580

5. 626, 628, 630, ____, ____

6. 450, 460, ____, ____, 490

7. 782, 784, ____, ____, 790

8. 803, 806, ____, ____, ____

CHALLENGE

If you start at 0, can you count by 4s to exactly 100? Why or why not?

Patterns with Numbers

1. Colour the even numbers green. This is an even number pattern.
   a. Give the pattern another name.

   ____

   b. Colour the odd numbers pink.

   ____

   c. What does the square look like now?

   ____

411	412	413	414	415
416	416	417	418	418
419	420	421	422	423
424	425	426	427	428
429	430	431	432	433

601	602	603	604	605
606	607	608	609	610
611				
			☆	

2. Write the numbers in the green boxes.
   a. Which number is above the star?

   ____

   b. Which number is to the left of the star?

   ____

   d. What is the last number in the table?

   ____

   e. Describe the pattern in the last column.

   ____

Skip counting

Read

Polly and Sam are having a snowball fight with their neighbours. Polly can make 20 snowballs from one bucket. Sam can throw 5 snowballs every minute.

Skip count to solve each problem.

1. Polly has 4 buckets of snow. How many snowballs can she make?

   5, 10, 15, 20, 25, 30, 35, 40, 45, 50, 55, 60, 65, 70, 75, 80

5, 10, 15, 20	25, 30, 35, 40	45, 50, 55, 60	65, 70, 75, 80
1st bucket	2nd bucket	3rd bucket	4th bucket

2. How many snowballs can Sam throw in 3 minutes?

   ____

3. Polly makes a total of 100 snowballs. How many buckets of snow did she scoop?

   ____

4. How many buckets of snow would Polly need to make 200 snowballs?

   ____

5. How long will it take Sam to throw 200 snowballs?

   ____

Tickle Your Brain!

Solve these Math puzzles and tickle your brain.

Draw a line across (---------------), up or down (I) or diagonally (X) to make 8 3-digit numbers.

Write the numbers in order from least to greatest.

____

____

3	1	2
4	0	5
9	6	8

Tell how you would use skip counting to find the number of:

- [ ] Fingers on 8 hands
- [ ] Tyres in 7 bicycles
- [ ] Sides on 5 triangles
- [ ] Toes on 7 people

Complete the chart.

345	
1. One less	
2. One hundred more	
3. Ten more	
4. One hundred less	

Fun with 3-digit Numbers

Look at the number cards.

7 4 8 5

1. Choose 3 cards and write:
   a. The largest number ___________
   b. The smallest number ___________
   c. An even number ___________
   d. An odd number ___________
   e. A number less than 780 ___________
   f. A number more than 450 ___________

2. a. Using the cards, write 5 different 3-digit numbers.

   ____

   b. Write the numbers from smallest to greatest.

   ____

3. Use the cards to write a number:
   a. Smaller than 245. ___________
   b. Greater than 562. ___________
   c. Between 510 and 570. ___________
   d. Two even numbers less than 732. ___________
   e. Two odd numbers more than 471. ___________

CHALLENGE

Which numbers from 100–500 read the same from left to right and right to left?

Rounding off Numbers

When we round off a number, we make it simpler by keeping its value close to the tens, hundreds or a higher place value.

For example: 17 can be rounded up to 20 and 23 can be rounded down to 20.

How to round off a number to the nearest 10?

- If the number you are rounding off has 5, 6, 7, 8 or 9, in the ones place, round the number up.

Example: 28 rounded off to the nearest 10 is 30.

- If the number you are rounding off has 0, 1, 2, 3 or 4 in the ones place, round the number down.

Example: 33 rounded off to the nearest 10 is 30.

Less than 5	More than 5
0 1 2 3 4	5 6 7 8 9
0	1

Rounding down ←— —→ Rounding up

CHALLENGE

To what number will you round off 98?

Will it be rounding off to the nearest 10 or 100?

Round Off to Nearest 10

The kids are playing with marbles. Round off each number they scored to the nearest 10.

Round	John	Kate	Neo
Round 1	9 →	34 →	12 →
Round 2	18 →	6 →	22 →
Round 3	11 →	20 →	31 →
Round 4	5 →	19 →	16 →
Round 5	18 →	39 →	27 →

Add the scores in each round and write the total. Round off to the nearest 10.

____

Round Off to Nearest 100

When rounding off to the nearest 100, look at the TENS DIGIT of the number.

- If that digit is 0, 1, 2, 3 or 4, round down to the previous 100.
- If that digit is 5, 6, 7, 8 or 9, round up to the next 100.

4**2**8 ≈ ? The tens digit is 2, so round down: 428 ≈ 400	7**7**1 ≈ ? The tens digit is 7, so round up: 771 ≈ 800	9**5**7 ≈ ? The tens digit is 5, so round up: 957 ≈ 1000

Round off these numbers to the nearest 100.

1.

616 ≈ ____________

327 ≈ ____________

2.

926 ≈ ____________

560 ≈ ____________

3.

470 ≈ ____________

867 ≈ ____________

4.

154 ≈ ____________

648 ≈ ____________

CHALLENGE

Whether you round up or down, the tens and ones digits change to zeros. True or false?

Rounding Off

Draw a ◯ around the number in each row that matches the description.

1.	rounds off to 30	23	37	34
2.	rounds off to 400	377	314	457
3.	rounds off to 80	85	72	83
4.	rounds off to 700	763	722	795
5.	rounds off to 50	57	48	59
6.	rounds off to 800	891	819	711
7.	rounds off to 60	56	67	69
8.	rounds off to 200	287	205	263
9.	rounds off to 300	346	368	351
10.	rounds off to 90	99	89	98

CHALLENGE

Find and tick any 3 numbers on the page that round off to 70.

Ordinal Numbers

Ordinal numbers tell us the position of an object in a series.

We further write ordinal numbers in this way:

21st – twenty first

34th – thirty fourth

56th – fifty sixth

63rd – sixty third

78th – seventy eighth

80th – eightieth

82nd – eighty second

99th – ninety ninth

100th – hundredth

116th – hundred and sixteenth

230th – two hundred and thirtieth

Ordinal Numbers

Study the picture of the building. Answer the questions.

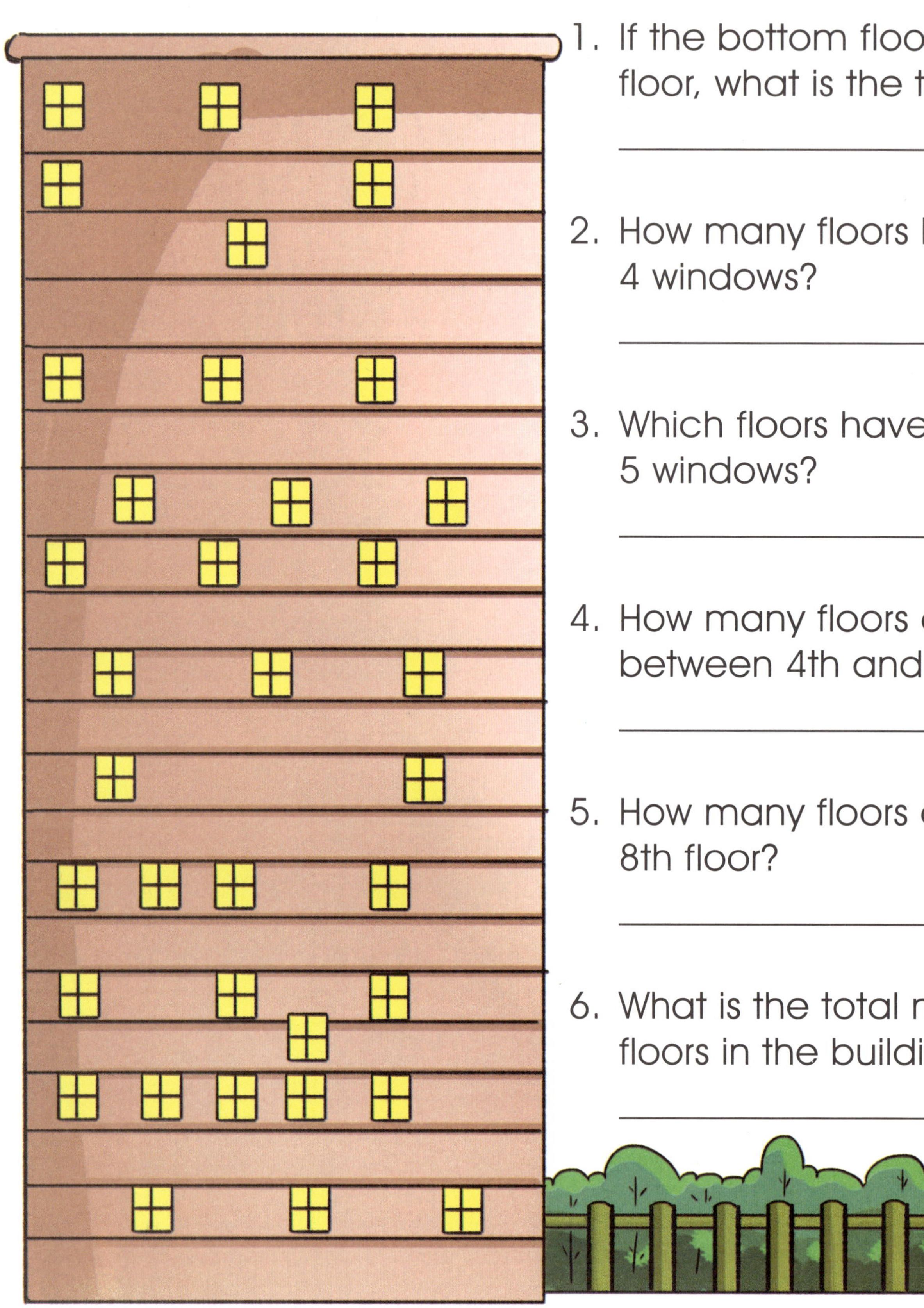

1. If the bottom floor is the 1st floor, what is the top floor?

   ____

2. How many floors have 4 windows?

   ____

3. Which floors have 5 windows?

   ____

4. How many floors are between 4th and 14th floor?

   ____

5. How many floors are above 8th floor?

   ____

6. What is the total number of floors in the building?

   ____

Ordinal Numbers

Read each problem and guess the position of animals.

Write their names in the correct order.

- Zebra is third. Giraffe is last. Hippo is second. Gorilla is in front of Hippo and Seal stands after Zebra.

____

- Giraffe is second. Gorilla is fifth. Seal comes before Gorilla. Zebra is in front of Giraffe. Hippo comes after Giraffe.

____

- Monkey is fourth. Elephant is second. Gorilla comes after Monkey. Hippo comes before. Elephant Giraffe stands before Monkey.

____

- Wolf is third. Fox is first. Rhino is fifth. Zebra is in front of Rhino. Kangaroo is behind Fox.

____

Answer Key

Page 2

1. 270, 420, 550, 700, 770, 920
2. 521, 522, 523, 524, 525, 526, 527, 528, 529
3. 275
4. 570
5. 520, 770, 920, 670

Page 3

From left to right :

1. 318, bedroom
2. 224, kitchen
3. 153, living room
4. 240, guest room
5. 165, bathroom
6. 419, family room
7. 351, dining room
8. 507, playroom

Page 4

Children will do on their own.

Page 5

From left to right

294, 507, 132, 625, 314, 850

Page 6

Before		After
338	339	340
516	517	518
207	208	209
898	899	900
699	700	701

	Between	
399	400	401
628	629	630
147	148	149
512	513	514
765	766	767
771	772	773

Page 7

a. 30 b. 30 c. 60

d. 100 e. 700 f. 800

g. 500 h. 10 i. 5

j. 0 k. 900 l. 9

m. 300 n. 2 o. 600

p. 50 q. 400 b. 40

Page 8

Children will do on their own.

Page 9

400 + 80 + 7

300 + 20 + 9

800 + 90 + 2

200 + 70 + 8

100 + 60 + 5

700 + 20 + 3

700 + 30 + 5

800 + 10 + 8

600 + 90 + 5

200 + 20 + 4

Answer Key

Page 10

1. 469	2. 678	3. 954
4. 809	5. 514	6. 629
7. 180	8 . 754	9. 388
10. 581	11. 273	12. 455
13. 199	14. 704	

Page 11

a. 764	b. 536	c. 818
d. 923	e. 438	f. 839
g. 503	h. 697	

Page 12

1. 322 < 434
2. 444 < 515
3. 613 > 612

Page 13

From left to right :

411, 809, 612

522, 891, 254 and 457

625, 218, 976

998, 786, 337

Page 14

1. No	2. Yes	3. No
4. No	5. Yes	6. Yes
7. No	8. Yes	

Page 15

1. 516, 561, 576
2. 324, 334, 343
3. 260, 602, 620
4. 101, 113, 131
5. 729, 734, 740
6. 800, 830, 893

Page 16

1. Six hundred and seventy nine
2. Three hundred and forty two
3. Nine hundred and eight
4. Five hundred and fifty six
5. Eight hundred and seventy six
6. Two hundred and fifty nine
7. Four hundred and forty five
8. One hundred and seventy eight
9. Seven hundred and eighty four
10. One hundred and nineteen

Page 17

a. 25	b. 35	c. 50
d. 5	e. 20	f. 45
g. 30	h. 15	i. 55
j. 40	k. 60	l . 10

Numbers from least to greatest:

5, 10, 15, 20, 25, 30, 35, 40, 45, 50, 55, 60

Numbers from largest to smallest:

105, 115, 125, 135, 145, 155, 165, 175, 185, 195, 205, 215, 225, 235, 245, 255, 265, 275

Answer Key

Page 18

1. 110, 120
2. 330
3. 229, 235
4. 560, 575
5. 632, 634
6. 470, 480
7. 786, 788
8. 809, 812, 815,

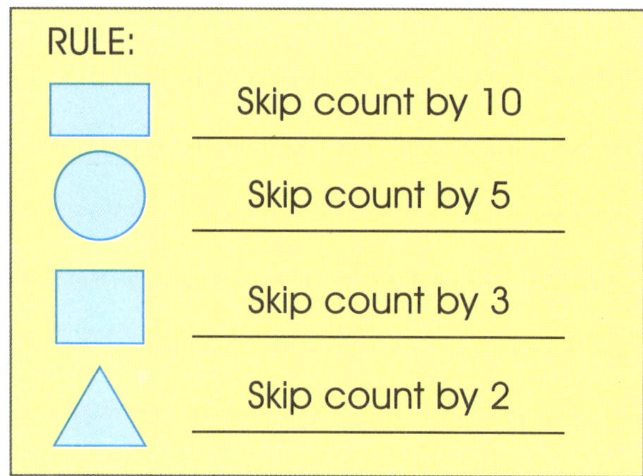

Page 19

Children will do on their own.

Page 20

2. 15
3. 5
4. 10
5. 40 minutes

Page 21

1. Children will do on their own.
2. 40, 14, 15, 70
3. 344, 445, 355, 245

Page 22

1 and 2 children will do on their own.

3.a. 244
b. 574, 585
c. 548
d. 724, 728
e. 485, 785

Page 24

Round 1: 10, 30, 10
Round 2: 20, 10, 20
Round 3: 10, 20, 30
Round 4: 10, 20, 20
Round 5: 20, 40, 30

Page 25

a. 600, 300
b. 900, 600
c. 500, 900
d. 200, 600

Page 26

a. 34
b. 377
c. 83
d. 722
e. 48
f. 819
g. 56
h. 205
i. 346
j. 89

Page 28

1. 21st
2. 2
3. 4th floor
4. 13 floors
5. 21

Page 29

1. Gorilla, hippo, zebra, seal, giraffe
2. Zebra, giraffe, hippo, seal, gorilla
3. Hippo, elephant, giraffe, monkey, gorilla
4. Fox, kangaroo, wolf, zebra, rhino